Fingerprinting

TEACHER'S GUIDE

Grades 4–8

Skills
Observing, Classifying, Drawing Conclusions,
Making Inferences

Concepts
Fingerprints, Standard Fingerprint Classification System,
Problem Solving

Science Themes
Systems & Interactions, Stability, Evolution,
Diversity & Unity

Mathematics Strands
Logic, Pattern

Nature of Science and Mathematics
Scientific Community, Interdisciplinary, Cooperative Efforts, Creativity &
Constraints, Theory-Based and Testable, Changing Nature of Facts and
Theories, Objectivity & Ethics, Science & Society, Real-Life Applications,
Science and Technology

Time
Three or four 30- to 60-minute sessions

Jeremy John Ahouse
Jacqueline Barber

LHS GEMS

Great Explorations in Math and Science (GEMS)
Lawrence Hall of Science
University of California at Berkeley

Illustrations
Carol Bevilacqua
Lisa Klofkorn

Photographs
Richard Hoyt, Jaine Kopp

Lawrence Hall of Science
University of California at Berkeley

Chairman: Glenn T. Seaborg
Director: Ian Carmichael

Initial support for the origination and publication of the GEMS series was provided by the A.W. Mellon Foundation and the Carnegie Corporation of New York. GEMS has also received support from the McDonnell-Douglas Foundation and the McDonnell-Douglas Employees Community Fund, the Hewlett Packard Company Foundation, and the people at Chevron USA. GEMS also gratefully acknowledges the contribution of word processing equipment from Apple Computer, Inc. This support does not imply responsibility for statements or views expressed in publications of the GEMS program. Under a grant from the National Science Foundation, GEMS Leader's Workshops have been held across the country. For further information on GEMS leadership opportunities, or to receive a publication brochure and the *GEMS Network News*, please contact GEMS at the address and phone number below.

International Standard Book Number: 0-924886-41-2

COMMENTS WELCOME

Great Explorations in Math and Science (GEMS) is an ongoing curriculum development project. GEMS guides are revised periodically, to incorporate teacher comments and new approaches. We welcome your criticisms, suggestions, helpful hints, and any anecdotes about your experience presenting GEMS activities. Your suggestions will be reviewed each time a GEMS guide is revised. Please send your comments to:
GEMS Revisions, c/o Lawrence Hall of Science, University of California, Berkeley, CA 94720. The phone number is (510) 642-7771.

Great Explorations in Math and Science (GEMS) Program

The Lawrence Hall of Science (LHS) is a public science center on the University of California at Berkeley campus. LHS offers a full program of activities for the public, including workshops and classes, exhibits, films, lectures, and special events. LHS is also a center for teacher education and curriculum research and development.

Over the years, LHS staff have developed a multitude of activities, assembly programs, classes, and interactive exhibits. These programs have proven to be successful at the Hall and should be useful to schools, other science centers, museums, and community groups. A number of these guided-discovery activities have been published under the Great Explorations in Math and Science (GEMS) title, after an extensive refinement process that includes classroom testing of trial versions, modifications to ensure the use of easy-to-obtain materials, and carefully written and edited step-by-step instructions and background information to allow presentation by teachers without special background in mathematics or science.

Staff

Glenn T. Seaborg, **Principal Investigator**
Jacqueline Barber, **Director**
Kimi Hosoume, **Assistant Director**
Cary Sneider, **Curriculum Specialist**
Katharine Barrett, Kevin Beals, Ellen Blinderman, Beatrice Boffen, John Erickson, Jaine Kopp, Laura Lowell, Linda Lipner, Debra Sutter, Rebecca Tilley, Laura Tucker, Carolyn Willard, **Staff Development Specialists**
Jan M. Goodman, **Mathematics Consultant**
Cynthia Eaton, **Administrative Coordinator**
Karen Milligan, **Distribution Coordinator**
Lisa Haderlie Baker, **Art Director**
Carol Bevilacqua and Lisa Klofkorn, **Designers**
Lincoln Bergman, **Principal Editor**
Carl Babcock, **Senior Editor**
Kay Fairwell, **Principal Publications Coordinator**
Nancy Kedzierski, Felicia Roston, Vivian Tong, Stephanie Van Meter, **Staff Assistants**

Contributing Authors

Jacqueline Barber	Linda Lipner	Susan Jagoda
Katharine Barrett	Laura Lowell	Larry Malone
Kevin Beals	Linda De Lucchi	Cary I. Sneider
Lincoln Bergman	Jean Echols	Debra Sutter
Celia Cuomo	Jan M. Goodman	Jennifer Meux White
Philip Gonsalves	Alan Gould	Carolyn Willard
Jaine Kopp	Kimi Hosoume	

Reviewers

We would like to thank the following educators who reviewed, tested, or coordinated the reviewing of this series of GEMS materials in manuscript form. Their critical comments and recommendations contributed significantly to these GEMS publications. Their participation does not necessarily imply endorsement of the GEMS program.

ARIZONA

Cheri Balkenbush
Shaw Butte Elementary School, Phoenix

Debbie Baratko
Shaw Butte Elementary School, Phoenix

Flo-Ann Barwick Campbell
Mountain Sky Junior High School, Phoenix

Nancy M. Bush
Desert Foothills Junior High School, Phoenix

Sandra Jean Caldwell
Lakeview Elementary School, Phoenix

George Casner
Desert Foothills Junior High School, Phoenix

Richard Clark*
Washington School District, Phoenix

Don Diller
Sunnyslope Elementary School, Phoenix

Carole Dunn
Lookout Mountain Elementary School, Phoenix

Joseph Farrier
Desert Foothills Junior High School, Phoenix

Robert E. Foster, III
Royal Palm Junior High School, Phoenix

Walter C. Hart
Desert View Elementary School, Phoenix

E.M. Heward
Desert Foothills Junior High School, Phoenix

Stephen H. Kleinz
Desert Foothills Junior High School, Phoenix

Karen Lee
Moon Mountain Elementary School, Phoenix

Nancy Oliveri
Royal Palm Junior High School, Phoenix

Susan Jean Parchert
Sunnyslope Elementary School, Phoenix

Brenda Pierce
Cholla Junior High School, Phoenix

C.R. Rogers
Mountain Sky Junior High School, Phoenix

Phyllis Shapiro
Sunset Elementary School, Glendale

David N. Smith
Maryland Elementary School, Phoenix

Leonard Smith
Cholla Junior High School, Phoenix

Sandra Stanley
Manzanita Elementary School, Phoenix

Roberta Vest
Mountain View Elementary School, Phoenix

CALIFORNIA

Richard Adams*
Montera Junior High School, Oakland

Gerald Bettman
Dan Mini Elementary School, Vallejo

Lee Cockrum*
Pennycook Elementary School, Vallejo

James A. Coley*
Dan Mini Elementary School, Vallejo

Deloris Parker Doster
Pennycook Elementary School, Vallejo

Jane Erni
Dan Mini Elementary School, Vallejo

Dawn Fairbanks
Columbus Intermediate School, Berkeley

Jose Franco
Columbus Intermediate School, Berkeley

Stanley Fukunaga
Montera Junior High School, Oakland

Ann Gilbert
Columbus Intermediate School, Berkeley

Karen E. Gordon
Columbus Intermediate School, Berkeley

Vana Lee James
Willard Junior High School, Berkeley

Dayle Kerstad*
Cave Elementary School, Vallejo

George J. Kodros
Piedmont High School, Piedmont

Jackson Lay*
Piedmont High School, Piedmont

Margaret Lacrampe
Sleepy Hollow Elementary School, Orinda

Chiyomi Masuda
Columbus Intermediate School, Berkeley

Kathy Nachbaur Mans
Pennycook Elementary School, Vallejo

Lin Morehouse*
Sleepy Hollow Elementary School, Orinda

Barbara Nagel
Montera Junior High School, Oakland

Neil Nelson
Cave Elementary School, Vallejo

Tina L. Nievelt
Cave Elementary School, Vallejo

Jeannie Osuna-MacIsaac
Columbus Intermediate School, Berkeley

Geraldine Piglowski
Cave Elementary School, Vallejo

Sandra Rhodes
Pennycook Elementary School, Vallejo

James Salak
Cave Elementary School, Vallejo

Aldean Sharp
Pennycook Elementary School, Vallejo

Bonnie Square
Cave Elementary School, Vallejo

Judy Suessmeier
Columbus Intermediate School, Berkeley

Phoebe A. Tanner
Columbus Intermediate School, Berkeley

Marc Tatar
University of California Gifted Program

Carolyn Willard*
Columbus Intermediate School

Robert L. Wood
Pennycook Elementary School, Vallejo

ILLINOIS

Sue Atac
Thayer J. Hill Junior High School, Naperville

Miriam Bieritz
Thayer J. Hill Junior High School, Naperville

Betty J. Cornell
Thayer J. Hill Junior High School, Naperville

Athena Digrindakis
Thayer J. Hill Junior High School, Naperville

Alice W. Dube
Thayer J. Hill Junior High School, Naperville

Kurt K. Engel
Waubonsie Valley High School, Aurora

Anne Hall
Thayer J. Hill Junior High School, Naperville

Linda Holdorf
Thayer J. Hill Junior High School, Naperville

Mardie Krumlauf
Thayer J. Hill Junior High School, Naperville

Lon Lademann
Thayer J. Hill Junior High School, Naperville

Mary Lou Lipscomb
Thayer J. Hill Junior High School, Naperville

Bernadine Lynch
Thayer J. Hill Junior High School, Naperville

Peggy E. McCall
Thayer J. Hill Junior High School, Naperville

Anne M. Martin
Thayer J. Hill Junior High School, Naperville

Elizabeth R. Martinez
Thayer J. Hill Junior High School, Naperville

Thomas G. Martinez
Waubonsie Valley High School, Aurora

Judy Mathison
Thayer J. Hill Junior High School, Naperville

Joan Maute
Thayer J. Hill Junior High School, Naperville

Mark Pennington
Waubonsie Valley High School, Aurora

Sher Renken*
Waubonsie Valley High School, Aurora

Judy Ronaldson
Thayer J. Hill Junior High School, Naperville

Michael Terronez
Waubonsie Valley High School, Aurora

KENTUCKY

Judy Allin
Rangeland Elementary School, Louisville

Martha Ash
Johnson Middle School, Louisville

Pamela Bayr
Johnson Middle School, Louisville

Pam Boykin
Johnson Middle School, Louisville

April Bond
Rangeland Elementary School, Louisville

Sue M. Brown
Newburg Middle School, Louisville

Jennifer L. Carson
Knight Middle School, Louisville

Lindagarde Dalton
Robert Frost Middle School, Louisville

Tom B. Davidson
Robert Frost Middle School, Louisville

Mary Anne Davis
Rangeland Elementary School, Louisville

John Dyer
Johnson Middle School, Louisville

Tracey Ferdinand
Robert Frost Middle School, Louisville

Jane L. Finan
Stuart Middle School, Louisville

Susan M. Freepartner
Knight Middle School, Louisville

Patricia C. Futch
Stuart Middle School, Louisville

Nancy L. Hack
Stuart Middle School, Louisville

Mildretta Hinkle
Johnson Middle School, Louisville

Barbara Hockenbury
Rangeland Elementary School, Louisville

Deborah M. Hornback
Museum of History and Science, Louisville

Nancy Hottman*
Newburg Middle School, Louisville

Brenda W. Logan
Newburg Middle School, Louisville

Amy S. Lowen*
Museum of History and Science, Louisville

Peggy Madry
Johnson Middle School, Louisville

Jacqueline Mayes
Knight Middle School, Louisville

Debbie Ostwalt
Stuart Middle School, Louisville

Gil Polston
Stuart Middle School, Louisville

Steve Reeves
Johnson Middle School, Louisville

Rebecca S. Rhodes
Robert Frost Middle School, Louisville

Patricia A. Sauer
Newburg Middle School, Louisville

Donna J. Stevenson
Knight Middle School, Louisville

Dr. William McLean Sudduth*
Museum of History and Science, Louisville

Carol Trussell
Rangeland Elementary School, Louisville

Janet W. Varon
Newburg Middle School, Louisville

Nancy Weber
Robert Frost Middle School, Louisville

MICHIGAN

John D. Baker
Portage North Middle School, Portage

Laura Borlik
Lake Michigan Catholic Elementary School, Benton Harbor

Sandra A. Burnett
Centreville Junior High School, Centreville

Colleen Cole
Comstock Northeast Middle School, Comstock

Sharon Christensen*
Delton-Kellogg Middle School, Delton

Beth Covey
The Gagie School, Kalamazoo

Ronald Collins
F.C. Reed Middle School, Bridgeman

Gary Denton
Gull Lake Middle School, Hickory Corners

Iola Dunsmore
Lake Center Elementary School, Portage

Margaret Erich
St. Monica Elementary School, Portage

Stirling Fenner
Gull Lake Middle School, Hickory Corners

Richard Fodor
F.C. Reed Middle School, Bridgeman

Daniel French
Portage North Middle School, Portage

Stanley L. Guzy
Bellevue Middle School, Bellevue

Dr. Alonzo Hannaford*
The Gagie School, Kalamazoo

Barbara Hannaford
The Gagie School, Kalamazoo

Karen J. Hileski
Comstock Northeast Middle School, Comstock

Suzanne Lahti
Lake Center Elementary School, Portage

Dr. Phillip T. Larsen*
Western Michigan University, Kalamazoo

Sandy Lellis
Bellevue Middle School, Bellevue

Betty Meyerink
F.C. Reed Middle School, Bridgeman

Rhea Fitzgerald Noble
Buchanan Middle School, Buchanan

John O'Toole
St. Monica Elementary School, Kalamazoo

Joan A. Rybarczyk
Lake Michigan Catholic Elementary School, Benton Harbor

Robert Underly
Buchanan Middle School, Buchanan

NEW YORK

Helene Berman
Webster Magnet Elementary School, New Rochelle

Robert Broderick
Trinity Elementary School, New Rochelle

Frank Capuzelo
Albert Leonard Junior High School, New Rochelle

Michael Colasuonno
Isaac E. Young Junior High School, New Rochelle

Antoinette DiGuglielmo
Webster Magnet Elementary School, New Rochelle

Linda Dixon
Scarsdale Junior High School, Scarsdale

Frank Faraone
Albert Leonard Junior High School, New Rochelle

Steven Frantz
Heathcote Elementary School, Scarsdale

Richard Golden*
Barnard School, New Rochelle

Seymour Golden
Albert Leonard Junior High School, New Rochelle

Lester Hallerman
Columbus Elementary School, New Rochelle

Vincent Iacovelli
Isaac E. Young Junior High School, New Rochelle

Cindy Klein
Columbus Elementary School, New Rochelle

Donna MacCrae
Webster Magnet Elementary School, New Rochelle

Robert Nebens
George M. Davis Elementary School, New Rochelle

Eileen Paolicelli
Ward Elementary School, New Rochelle

Dr. John V. Pozzi*
City School District of New Rochelle, New Rochelle

John Russo
Ward Elementary School, New Rochelle

Bruce Seiden
Webster Magnet Elementary School, New Rochelle

David Selleck
Albert Leonard Junior High School, New Rochelle

Charles Yochim
George M. Davis Elementary School, New Rochelle

Bruce Zeller
Isaac E. Young Junior High School, New Rochelle

*Trial test coordinators

Contents

Acknowledgments

The technique of fingerprinting using pencil, paper, and tape was described in the *Skin Prints* module, part of the Health Activities Project (HAP K–3), developed at the Lawrence Hall of Science. The fingerprinting activities described in this unit are part of a series of crime lab science activities developed and presented by the Lawrence Hall of Science Chemistry Education Program. Jeremy Ahouse, the author of this version, was assisted by Jacqueline Barber in writing the "Fingerprinting" unit.

Introduction

Fingerprints demonstrate both the uniqueness and the commonality of human beings. They are infinitely varied but fall into specific categories. As such, fingerprinting is an ideal tool for learning and practicing observation and classification skills.

The fingers-on activities in this unit allow you and your students to explore the similarities and variations of fingerprints. Your students become criminalists as they use the standard fingerprint classification scheme to solve a crime. But before the crime can be solved, students explore the intricacies of fingerprints by taking their own prints, devising their own methods of classification, and practicing classification with the standard system.

Teachers have found this unit to be an ideal lead-in to a variety of interesting follow-up activities. These ideas are listed in the "Going Further" section on page 28. Your students will undoubtedly be full of questions about fingerprints and their uses. "Behind the Scenes" on page 31 includes answers to typical student questions, such as, "Who keeps track of fingerprints?" "How do the police remove fingerprints from the scene of a crime?" and "Can a person change or remove her fingerprints?" So, put on your criminalist's cap, get out your magnifying lens, and have fun with fingerprinting.

One of the "Going Further" activities, on page 30, suggests creating your own mysteries. While this guide provides one mystery scenario with characters, we strongly encourage you to create one of your own, perhaps with a familiar classroom or school setting, and characters, or by making use of fictional characters or caricatured real-life celebrity-types that may be of more interest to your students. Depending on the age and background of your students, you may also want to stress that the "crimes" are pretend ones, and that "any resemblance" to real persons or events is, as the phrase goes, "purely coincidental." Once students have become familiar with fingerprinting and its uses in solving a mystery, the class can work in groups to come up with their own imaginative scenarios with which to challenge other classes. A blank version of the "Suspect Sheet" is provided in the back of the book for your convenience in creating your own mysteries.

If your students enjoy these activities, we highly recommend that you pursue the mystery motif by presenting other GEMS activities. In Crime Lab Chemistry, students use the chemical technique of paper chromatography to investigate which pen was used to write an imaginary ransom note. In the GEMS guide Mystery Festival, scheduled to be published in late 1993, students at classroom learning stations conduct numerous scientific tests on evidence to attempt to solve a mystery. Mystery Festival includes two different mysteries: for younger and older students. In addition to the hands-on activities, and much practice analyzing evidence and differentiating evidence from inference, these GEMS guides demonstrate how working together to solve mysteries can be very directly compared to the process of scientific investigation.

Time Frame

Session 1: Making Fingerprints
    Teacher Preparation: 25 minutes
    Classroom Activity: 30–45 minutes

Session 2: Classifying Fingerprints
    Teacher Preparation: 15 minutes
    Classroom Activity: 45–60 minutes

Session 3: Solving the Crime
    Teacher Preparation: 10 minutes
    Classroom Activity: 25–40 minutes

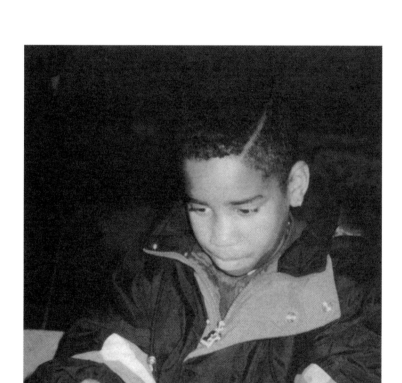

What You Need *(for all sessions)*

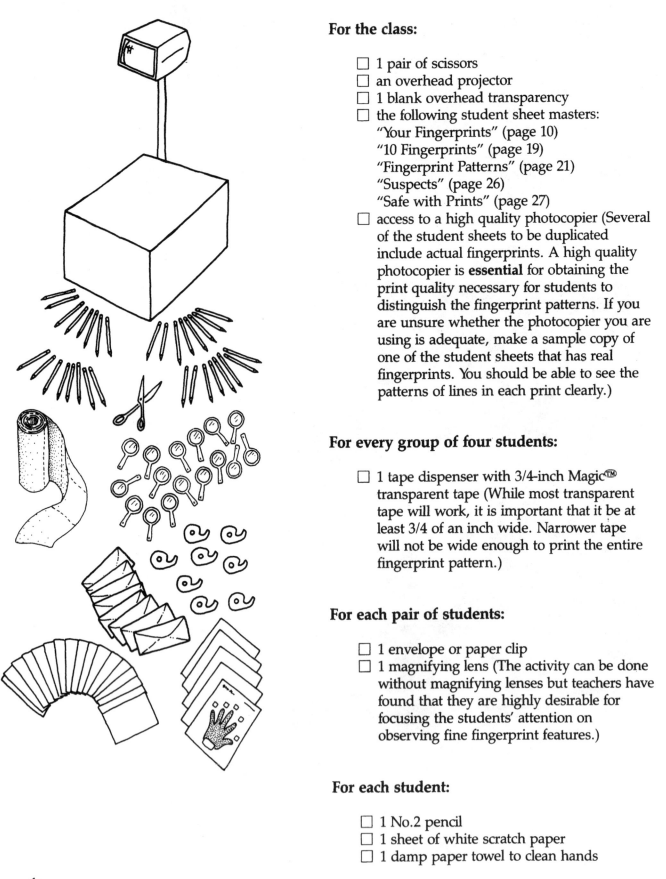

For the class:

- ☐ 1 pair of scissors
- ☐ an overhead projector
- ☐ 1 blank overhead transparency
- ☐ the following student sheet masters:
  "Your Fingerprints" (page 10)
  "10 Fingerprints" (page 19)
  "Fingerprint Patterns" (page 21)
  "Suspects" (page 26)
  "Safe with Prints" (page 27)
- ☐ access to a high quality photocopier (Several
  of the student sheets to be duplicated
  include actual fingerprints. A high quality
  photocopier is **essential** for obtaining the
  print quality necessary for students to
  distinguish the fingerprint patterns. If you
  are unsure whether the photocopier you are
  using is adequate, make a sample copy of
  one of the student sheets that has real
  fingerprints. You should be able to see the
  patterns of lines in each print clearly.)

For every group of four students:

- ☐ 1 tape dispenser with 3/4-inch Magic™
  transparent tape (While most transparent
  tape will work, it is important that it be at
  least 3/4 of an inch wide. Narrower tape
  will not be wide enough to print the entire
  fingerprint pattern.)

For each pair of students:

- ☐ 1 envelope or paper clip
- ☐ 1 magnifying lens (The activity can be done
  without magnifying lenses but teachers have
  found that they are highly desirable for
  focusing the students' attention on
  observing fine fingerprint features.)

For each student:

- ☐ 1 No.2 pencil
- ☐ 1 sheet of white scratch paper
- ☐ 1 damp paper towel to clean hands

Getting Ready (for all sessions)

1. Duplicate one copy of the following two student sheets for each student: "Your Fingerprints" and "Fingerprint Patterns" from the masters on pages 10 and 21.

2. Use a high quality photocopier to duplicate one "10 Fingerprints" sheet from the master on page 19, for each pair of students. Photocopy one "Suspects" sheet and one "Safe with Prints" sheet for each student from the masters on pages 26 and 27.

3. Make an overhead transparency of the "Fingerprint Patterns" sheet from the master on page 21. While using an overhead projector in this activity may seem optional, teachers have found that it significantly increases students' understanding of how to classify fingerprints.

4. Before you begin the unit, spend 5-10 minutes learning the fingerprinting technique described on page 8 by making your own set of fingerprints.

5. Sometime before beginning Session 2, cut out the ten fingerprints from the "10 Fingerprints" sheets and put them together in an envelope. Make one envelope containing all ten prints for each pair of students. Alternatively, you can have the students cut out the fingerprints. Teachers who present this activity many times to different groups of students have chosen to laminate the ten fingerprints.

6. Also before Session 2, familiarize yourself with the standard fingerprint classification scheme by reading the descriptions of the main categories on the "Fingerprint Patterns" sheet on page 21. Practice classifying the "10 Fingerprints." Check yourself with the key for "10 Fingerprints" on page 20. Try classifying your own fingerprints. As you attempt to classify more and more fingerprints, you will discover that many prints seem to fit in more than one category. Your job in classifying them is to decide, for instance, whether *most* of the lines "leave" on the same side of the print that they "started" (like a loop), or whether *most* of the lines "leave" on the other side of the print (like an arch).

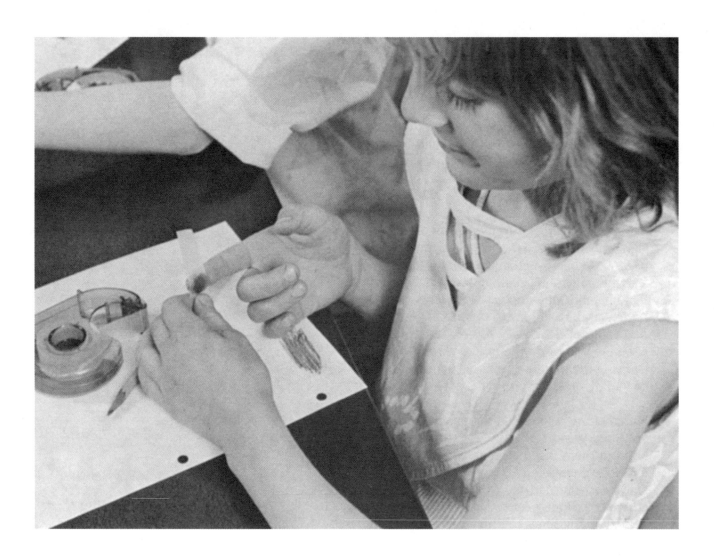

Session 1: Making Fingerprints

In this session, your students are introduced to fingerprints. They learn a method for taking their own fingerprints, using pencil, paper, and tape. After practicing the technique, they place a set of their fingerprints on their "Your Fingerprints" sheets.

What You Need

For every group of four students:
- ☐ 1 tape dispenser with tape

For each student:
- ☐ 1 No.2 pencil
- ☐ 1 sheet of white scratch paper
- ☐ 1 "Your Fingerprints" data sheet (master on page 10)
- ☐ 1 damp paper towel to clean hands

Introducing the Activity

1. Lead the class in a short discussion of fingerprints by asking:

- "What are fingerprints?"

- "Raise your hand if you've heard that all people's fingerprints are different."

- "Have you had your fingerprints taken?"

- "What are some of the reasons fingerprints are taken?"

- "Why are prints taken from fingers — couldn't we take elbow or ankle prints instead?" [One logical response is that fingers are used to pick things up.]

2. Tell your students that they will become **criminalists** in this unit. Criminalists are people who study crimes and analyze clues in a systematic and scientific way. Fingerprints are an important part of what criminalists study, and that is what your students will be doing, starting with their own fingerprints.

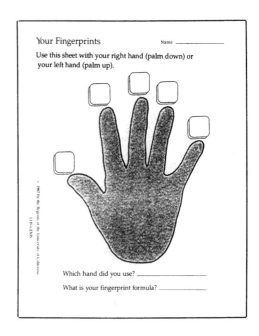

Your Fingerprints   Name _____

Use this sheet with your right hand (palm down) or your left hand (palm up).

Which hand did you use? _____

What is your fingerprint formula? _____

A criminalist is a person who uses science to analyze physical evidence in legal proceedings. Another name for a criminalist is a forensic scientist. A criminologist is a social scientist who studies why people commit crimes and how crime can be prevented.

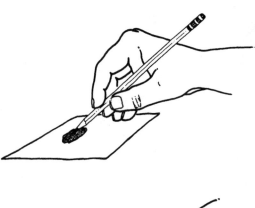

Practicing Making Prints

1. Show the students how to take fingerprints:

   a.) Using a No. 2 pencil, rub a small black patch of graphite onto a piece of paper.

   b.) Rub your finger back and forth across the graphite. It is important that the **front** of the finger, **not** the tip, be blackened. If only the tip is blackened the print will not include the "interesting" part of the fingerprint. The "interesting" part of the print can be seen by looking at the front of your finger. The area between the tip and the bend at the first knuckle has lines that swirl, loop, arch, or in some other way have a pattern. You may want to have your students practice locating the center of the print. Ask everyone to place their pencil point in the center of the print, halfway between the bend of their first knuckle and the tip of their finger.

   c.) After your finger is blackened, use a piece of tape to "lift" the fingerprint directly from the finger. Have your students place the bottom edge of the tape on the line of the first joint. (Make a simple drawing on the board which shows the tape going across the front of the finger.)

   d.) Finally, place the tape on a clean part of the white scratch paper. The fingerprint can now be seen and examined.

2. Warn the students **not** to make their fingerprints **too dark,** as this makes them very difficult to read. One way to avoid this is to point out that the graphite mark on the scratch paper need not be too dark. Using the same graphite patch to print all fingers will help keep the prints from becoming too dark.

   Also, encourage your students to use paper towels to keep their fingers clean. This will keep the tape from getting smudged.

3. Ask the students to start by making a few practice prints. You may want to ask them to make one print that's too dark, one print that's too light, and one print that's smudgy. The goal is to let them practice until they can make clear prints.

4. Distribute a pencil and a piece of scratch paper to each student and a tape dispenser to each group of four students, and let them begin practicing.

5. Go around the room and help, making sure that:

- the prints are coming from the front of the finger, not the tip,

- the tape is not wrinkled, and

- the fingerprints are not too dark.

Always examine the prints after the tape has been placed on the paper, as it is much easier to see them this way. When all of your students can make clear prints, go to the next step.

Making a Clean Set of Fingerprints

1. Hold up a "Your Fingerprints" sheet and tell the students to each make a set of very clean prints and stick them to their sheets. Show them how they can use either their right hand (palm down) or their left hand (palm up). Ask them to record on their sheet which hand they use.

2. Distribute a "Your Fingerprints" sheet to each student and have them get started.

3. Encourage the students to make the best set of prints possible. If someone "messes up" it is easy to start over. Just remove the print by peeling the tape off the paper. Circulate around the room as the students work, and help them make clear prints.

Left   or   Right

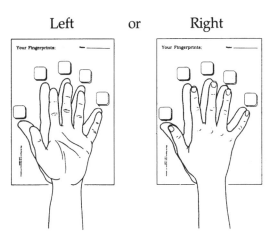

4. Give magnifying lenses to students who finish early, and have them examine their prints carefully. When all of the students are done, collect the fingerprint sheets.

5. Tell the students that in the next session they will have a chance to examine their fingerprints much more closely.

Your Fingerprints

Use this sheet with your right hand (palm down) or
your left hand (palm up).

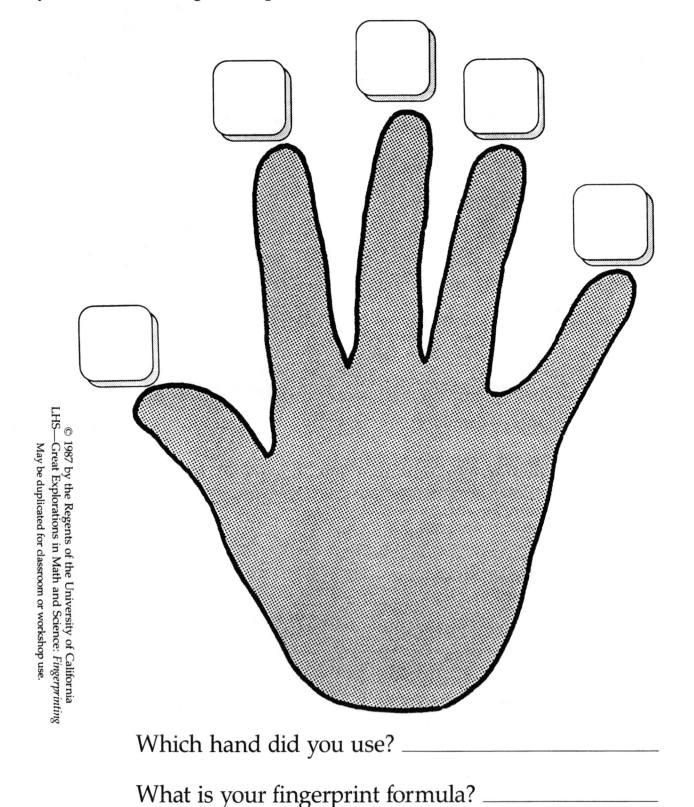

Which hand did you use? _____

What is your fingerprint formula? _____

Your Fingerprints (Example)

Name <u>Kim Anderson</u>

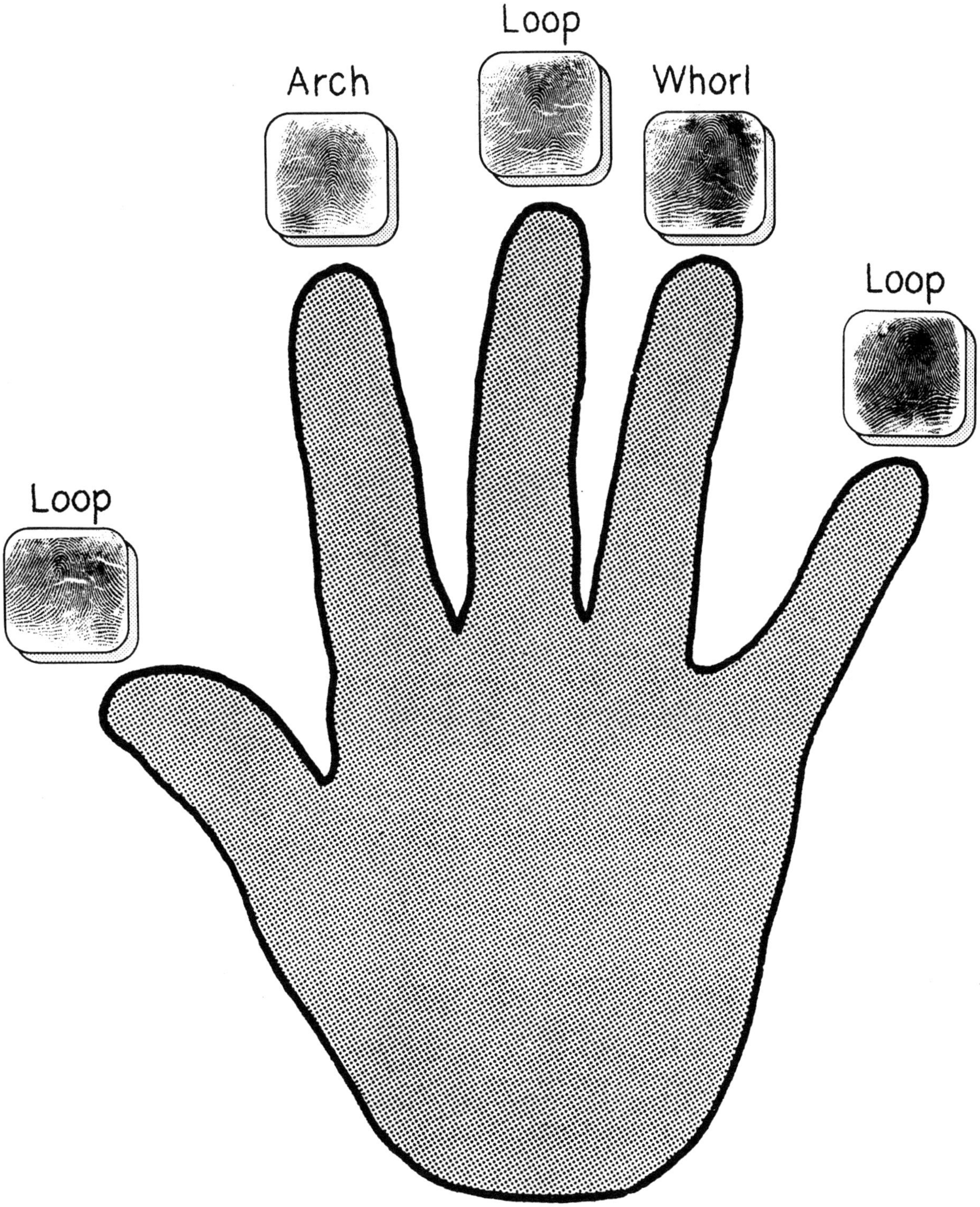

Arch

Loop

Whorl

Loop

Loop

Which hand did you use? <u>Right</u>

What is your fingerprint formula? <u>L-A-L-W-L</u>

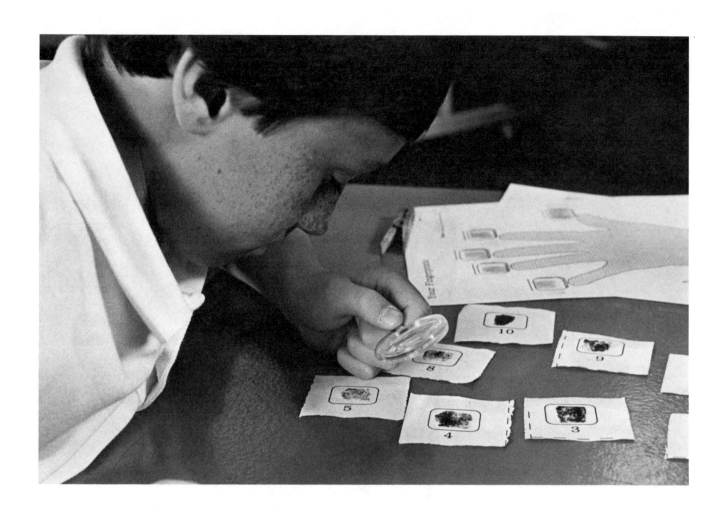

Session 2: Classifying Fingerprints

In this session, the students group ten different fingerprints according to how they look, to create their own scheme for classifying prints. Then they are introduced to a "standard" system of fingerprint classification, the arch-loop-whorl system. They practice using this system, and apply it to their own prints from Session 1 to get their "fingerprint formulas."

The first part of Session 2 is very important. Your students are defining their own descriptive categories and applying them. Make sure to give them enough time to explore this fully.

What You Need

For the class:
- ☐ 1 pair of scissors
- ☐ 1 overhead transparency of "Fingerprint Patterns"
- ☐ an overhead projector

For each pair of students:
- ☐ 1 envelope containing the "10 Fingerprints" (See "Getting Ready" #5 on page 5.)
- ☐ 2 "Fingerprint Patterns" sheets (master on page 21)
- ☐ a magnifying lens

For each student:
- ☐ a completed "Your Fingerprints" sheet from Session 1
- ☐ a pencil

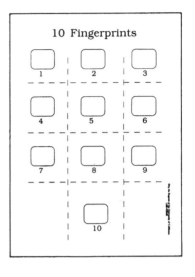

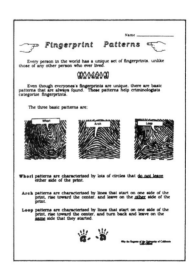

Larger versions of the three main fingerprint patterns are provided at the back of this book should you wish to use them for transparencies.

Students Create Their Own Fingerprint Classifications

1. Review by asking the students to describe what they did in the first session. Explain that in this session they will learn more about fingerprints. Divide the class into pairs of students.

2. Show the students an envelope containing the ten fingerprints. Explain that each team will get a set of these ten prints. Tell the students that they may use magnifying lenses to examine the prints more carefully.

3. Tell your students to look at the ten fingerprint patterns and think of words to describe what they see. Distribute the packets of ten fingerprints and the magnifying lenses. Let the students have several minutes to examine the prints.

4. Ask the students to share words that describe the patterns of lines in the fingerprints. Record their "descriptions" on the board. Accept and record *all* of the responses. Typical student descriptions include: rainbow, bulls-eye, square, maze, coiled, dark, circular, swirling, wave, and tornado. The goal is to involve your students in examining and describing the lines that make up a fingerprint.

5. Explain that criminalists must be able to pick out one particular fingerprint out of thousands of fingerprints. To do this they have to find ways to group them. Ask the students to sort the ten fingerprints into groups. The students may choose to make as many or as few groups as they'd like.

6. Walk around and encourage the students. If a team has difficulty getting started, give them an example: If we wanted to sort all of the shoes in this room, we could do it in several ways. We could put all of the tie shoes in one pile, the buckle shoes in a different pile, and the slip-on shoes in a third pile. How else could we sort the shoes? [By color, by size, etc.]

7. Ask pairs of students why they grouped the prints the way they did. Typical responses include: "These are hills," "These are waves," "These have waves over triangles," "These are circles," and "This has little humps." Encourage the students to be imaginative.

8. After the students have sorted their prints, reconvene the group and ask, "Which prints did you group with print #1?" Write several groups' responses on the board. Ask the students to explain why they grouped a particular print with print #1. You can do this with other prints, for five to ten minutes, depending on the students' level of interest. Some teachers have had their students write descriptions of the categories they created.

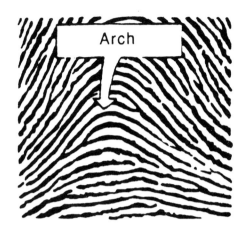

Learning the Standard Fingerprint Classification System

1. Tell the students that criminalists have also devised a way to sort or classify fingerprints. Use the overhead and the transparency to show the three patterns to the whole class.

2. Define the three basic fingerprint types:

- *arches* have lines that start on one side, rise, and exit on the other side of the print

- *loops* have lines that enter and exit on the same side of the print

- *whorls* have circles that do not exit on either side of the print.

If possible, relate the "standard" categories to categories that the students generated. For instance, "The 'arch' group seems to be just a different name for what Steve and Lisa called their 'rainbow' group."

3. Explain that some prints might seem to fit in either of two groups. For example, a print might have some lines that start on one side and exit on the other side of the print (like an arch) and other lines that enter and exit on the same side of the print (like a loop). Tell the students that they will need to decide whether **most** of the lines are like the lines in an arch or whether most of them are like the lines in a loop. Ask the students if they have any questions.

Applying the Standard Classification

1. Ask the students to use the arch/loop/whorl system to classify the ten prints that they had previously classified on their own. Walk around the room and help, as needed.

2. After the students have classified the fingerprints, go to the board and write the three headings, "arch," "loop," and "whorl."

3. Under these headings list the numbered prints by asking, "Which prints did you think were arches?" Write the students' responses on the board.

4. After all of the responses are listed on the board, identify a number that is listed under more than one heading. Lead a short discussion to decide in which category that print fits best. If there is a lot of contention and the class can't decide, ask if they think a new category needs to be invented.

It's not only okay for your students to struggle with the task of classifying hard-to-classify prints, but such discussions are important in developing their understanding of both the standard fingerprint classifications and of the process of classifying. The goal is not to force all the students to agree on a particular categorization, but rather to **clarify and refine the definitions of each category** so that it will be easier to classify individual prints.

arch	loop	whorl
8,6,1,7	7,3,10	9,2,3
9,4,2	5,4,9,2	5

IMPORTANT NOTE: Some of the fingerprints that do not fit easily into the three categories are sometimes put into a fourth category called "mixed." An unusual fingerprint is included in the set of ten. Encourage the students to grapple with this print using their own classifications and the standard system. If your students find shortcomings in the system encourage *them* to suggest solutions. Go ahead and present the fourth category of "mixed" only after your students have considered all other options. Introducing this new category too early often results in students placing all hard-to-classify prints in it. If this becomes a problem, come up with a rule for when it's okay to call a print "mixed."

5. Ask three students to describe each of the three basic fingerprint categories "in their own words."

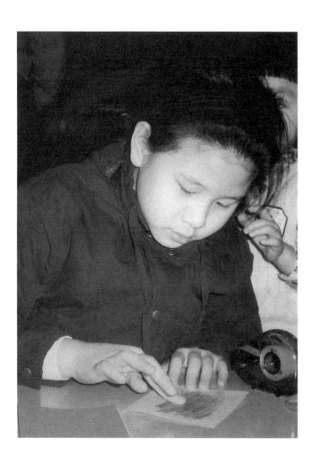

If there are fingerprints that stump several students, you could have them print these fingers again, and stick the tape with the print directly on a blank overhead transparency. This way you can project the problem print so everyone can see it at the same time. Have the class discuss how to classify it.

There are many more refined classification schemes. Students can do research to learn more about radial loops (that open toward the thumb) and ulnar loops (that open toward the little finger). Some classification schemes refer to plain arches and tented arches. Eight main different patterns of ridges (the raised lines that make up the print pattern) have also been identified.

For an excellent math extension, you could help the class create a class histogram, or graphic representation, of the distribution of their fingerprint types. Older students could also devise graphs that are able to track the distinctions within the three main types, to indicate, for example, if an arch, loop, or whorl goes to the right or left, as well as other more elaborate classification schemes.

Finding Their Own Fingerprint Formulas

1. Now have the students classify their own prints, using the standard classification system. Distribute the "Your Fingerprints" sheets from the first session. Students who finish quickly can double-check their classifications or help another student who is unsure.

2. When all of the students finish, tell them that you'd like them to figure out their "fingerprint formulas." A fingerprint formula is the list of print classifications for one hand, **from thumb to pinkie.** For example, a hand that has fingers of loop, arch, arch, whorl, loop, has a formula of **l-a-a-w-l.** Ask each student to write his fingerprint formula at the bottom of his "Your Fingerprints" sheet.

3. Ask the students to trade data sheets with their teammates and check each other's classifications. If the teammates disagree, encourage them to discuss their opinions with one another.

4. End this session by asking a few students to tell the class their fingerprint formulas.

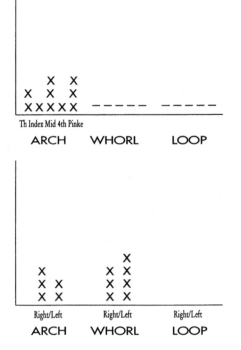

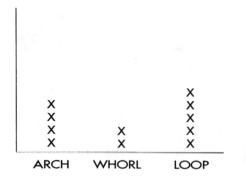

10 Fingerprints

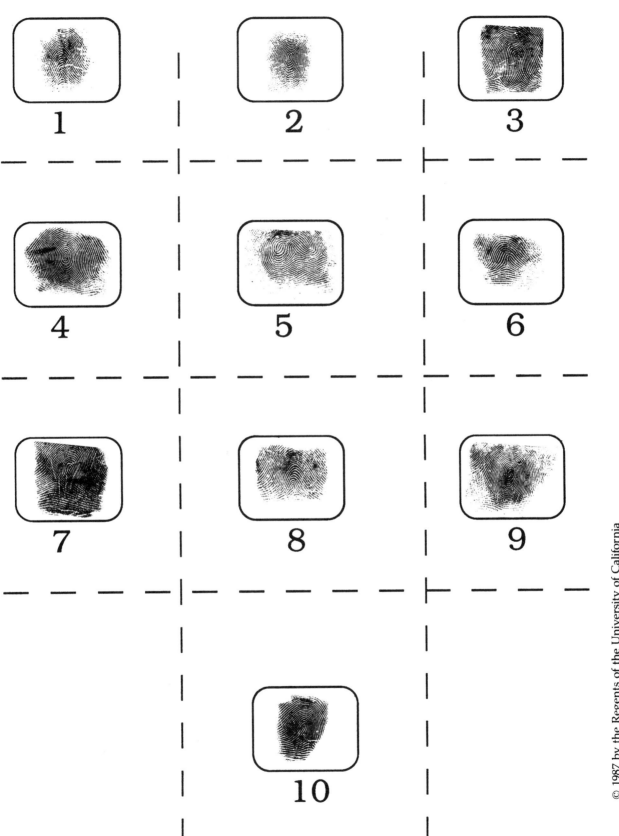

10 Fingerprints Key

arch 1	whorl 2	loop 3
whorl 4	mixed 5	arch 6
loop 7	arch 8	whorl 9
	loop 10	

This is the key to the student sheet for Session 2, "Classifying Fingerprints." (Remember that these categories are not absolute.)

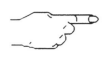 # Fingerprint Patterns

Every person in the world has a unique set of fingerprints, unlike those of any other person who ever lived.

Even though everyone's fingerprints are unique, there are basic patterns that are always found. These patterns help criminalists classify fingerprints.

The three basic patterns are:

 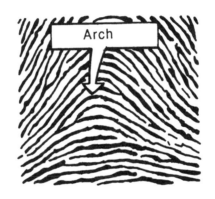 

Whorl patterns have lots of circles that **do not leave** either side of the print.

Arch patterns have lines that start on one side of the print, rise toward the center, and leave on the **other** side of the print.

Loop patterns have lines that start on one side of the print, rise toward the center, turn back and leave on the **same** side from which they started.

Session 3: Solving the Crime

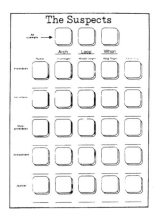

The Suspects

The students solve a mystery by using the standard classification system introduced in Session 2. They are given the suspects' fingerprints, the formula of the fingerprints found at the scene of the crime, and finally, copies of the actual prints.

What You Need

For each student:
- [ ] 1 "Suspects" student sheet (master on page 26)
- [ ] 1 "Safe with Prints" (master on page 27)
- [ ] 1 pencil
- [ ] 1 magnifying lens

Safe with prints

Who Robbed the Safe?

1. Tell the students to imagine that a crime has been committed. It is time to use what they have learned about fingerprints to try and solve the crime. Explain that a safe has been robbed. The safe is in the office of the president of a big company, and was found early this morning open and empty. The theft was discovered by the night security guard. The guard called the police immediately. There are five suspects:

- *Barbie Brilliant,* the president of the company, is in debt, owing money to many people.

- *Stewart Starr,* the vice-president, has been trying to take over control of the company.

- *Peter Page,* the secretary, was recently fired unfairly. He left without returning the keys to the building.

- *Ned Numbers,* the accountant, has three cars, a big house, and lives very luxuriously.

- *Carla Clean,* the janitor, was recently injured on the job and wasn't given any days off to recuperate. She is very angry about this.

Barbie Brilliant

Stewart Starr

Peter Page

Ned Numbers

Carla Clean

2. Hold up a copy of the "Suspects" sheet. Tell the students that these are the fingerprints of the suspects' right hands. The fingerprints found on the safe were from a right hand. Explain that when the police first investigate evidence, they narrow down the number of suspects by comparing the suspects' fingerprint formulas to the formula of prints found as evidence.

3. Tell your students that their first task will be to find the fingerprint formulas of the five suspects. You will give them the formula of the prints found on the safe after they have figured out the fingerprint formula of each suspect. This serves as a review and practice of the standard classification system. There are examples of the categories at the top of the data sheet, for those students who have forgotten what they look like. [Two of the formulas match the fingerprint formula on the safe.]

4. Distribute a "Suspects" sheet to each student and have them begin. Answer questions about the classifications and help the students determine the fingerprint formulas.

5. After all of the students have figured out the suspects' fingerprint formulas, reveal the fingerprint formula of the prints found on the safe: **l-a-l-w-l** (thumb to pinkie), or loop, arch, loop, whorl, loop.

6. Let the students speculate on "who done it." Ask which suspects they can now eliminate, based on this evidence.

7. Now distribute the "Safe with Prints" sheet.

8. Ask the students to decide whose prints are on the safe. (They will be making a one-to-one comparison of the prints and will probably be able to do this very quickly.) Ask students who finish early to determine whether they have the same fingerprint formula as the one that appeared on the safe.

Evaluating the Evidence

1. Ask the students to tell you which of the suspects has prints that match those on the safe. Also ask them to give you reasons why they think that the others do not match. Encourage very specific answers. Some teachers have had their students write a description of the evidence and what led them to believe it was a certain suspect's prints on the safe.

2. After the students have decided whose prints are on the safe, ask whether or not these prints might normally be on the safe, or if finding the prints proves that the suspect they identified robbed the safe. One of the goals of this series of activities is to let students gather evidence and draw conclusions from the evidence. Who actually robbed the safe is less important than the *process* your students used to arrive at their conclusions. By the way, it was the accountant's prints that were found on the safe, but we still don't know who robbed the safe. While the accountant may have needed the money, there are lots of legitimate reasons why his fingerprints might be on the safe!

3. Ask the students if there are any other techniques they can think of that they, as detectives, could use to help solve this crime.

Suspects

An Example →

Arch	Loop	Whorl

	Thumb	Forefinger	Middle finger	Ring finger	Little finger
President					
Secretary					
Vice-President					
Accountant					
Janitor					

Safe with prints

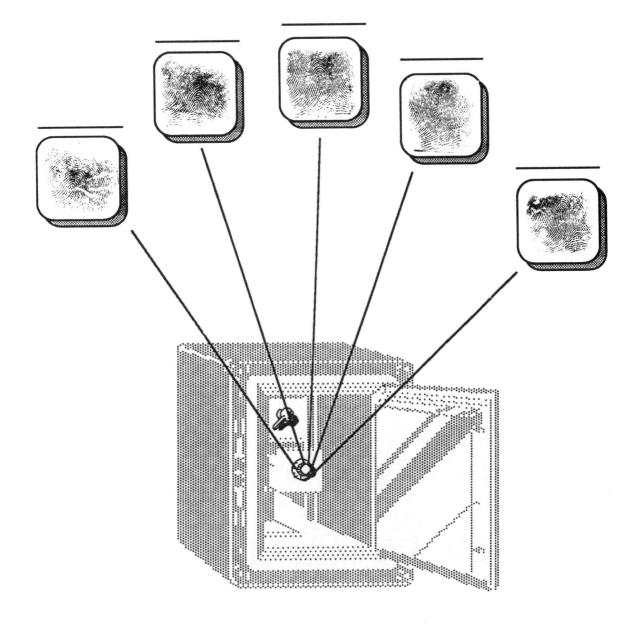

Going Further

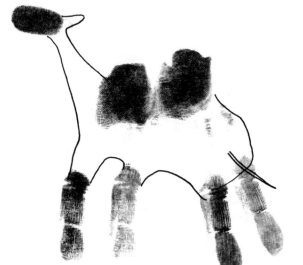

Crime Lab Chemistry

If you and your students enjoyed this unit, consider presenting the GEMS unit on *Crime Lab Chemistry*. In *Crime Lab Chemistry*, the students use the chemical technique of paper chromatography to determine which black pen was used to write a ransom note. Your students will get further practice in gathering evidence and making inferences while learning about pigments, solubility, and techniques used to separate mixtures.

Fingerprints as an Introduction

Fingerprints are a wonderful example of the variations among people. The activities in this unit can be used as a lead-in to subsequent activities in biology (the human body, animal skin types), genetics (find out if your students have fingerprints like their parents or siblings), criminology, and evidence gathering.

Fingerprint Trends

After Session 2, "Classifying Fingerprints," find out which prints occur most frequently in your class. Have your students make bar graphs to represent this data.

Do Identical Twins Have Identical Fingerprints?

Find out! Locate a pair of identical twins at your school or in your community. Take their fingerprints and have your students decide the answer to this question for themselves.

Toe Prints

As a homework assignment, have your students print their toes and classify them according to the arch/loop/whorl system.

Fingerprint Art

Let your students use ink pads to make pictures with prints from their hands. Lots of little fingerprints can look like flowers. Full-finger prints and thumbs can create an underwater world of seaweed and fish. The meaty part or bottom of a fist can make a print that looks like an elephant's trunk.

More Complex Classifications

Scott Foresman Intermediate Dictionary defines the eight categories of fingerprints used by criminalists: plain arch, left loop, right loop, plain whorl, double loop, tented arch, central pocket loop, and accidental. Scars and wrinkles may also be used to categorize fingerprints. Ask your students to research the history of fingerprints and classification schemes.

News Reporters

As a language arts extension, have your students write newspaper articles about the crime in Session 3, draw pictures and create stories about each of the suspects.

Mystery Books

Some teachers have presented these fingerprint activities as part of a mystery reading unit.

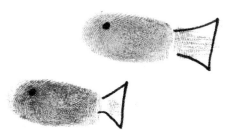

One teacher, for example, created imaginary "suspects" in a mystery from popular songs ("Bad" by Michael Jackson, "Charlie Brown" by the Coasters, "Born in East L.A." by Cheech Marin, etc.) then played the songs during the week prior to the activity. Students jotted down notes on the suspects as they listened to the songs.

Fingerprinting can provide a great opportunity for classes to exchange and compare data over a computer network. Here's an interesting histogram supplied by a teacher over just such a network, which is based on real Scotland Yard data, and shows fingerprint type occurrence for a sample of 5000 people. Scotland Yard classifies two types of loops (radial and ulnar).

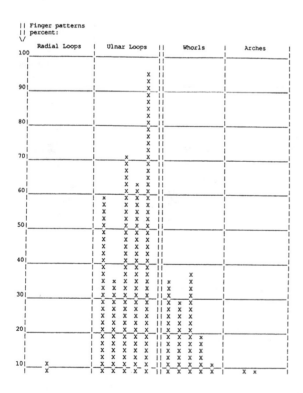

Create Your Own Mystery

Construct a fun classroom mystery for your students to solve—who was the last person to use the pencil sharpener? Privately arrange with a student who is willing to be the "culprit," to give you a set of her fingerprints. Compile a group of suspects. Have your students determine the fingerprint formulas of the suspects. Then reveal the formula of prints "found on the pencil sharpener." For an unexpected twist, have the culprit be the janitor, principal, or some other person at the school who is not a member of your class. More complex mysteries can be created using partial prints or more than one person's prints.

Find My Thumb (a game)

Ask every student to make a print of his thumb on two index cards. Have each student place one index card, labelled with his name, face up on his desk and give the other card (unlabelled) to you. Shuffle the unidentified index cards and then pass them out to students. Ask the students to try to find the person whose thumb print they have been given.

Classifications and Exponents

For older students, introduce the idea of the number of possible combinations that a given classification scheme gives. For example with three classifications (arch, loop, and whorl) there are $3 \times 3 \times 3 \times 3 \times 3 = 3^5$ or 243 different fingerprint formulas possible for one hand. If we add a fourth category (like a combination arch-loop), then we have $4 \times 4 \times 4 \times 4 \times 4 = 4^5$ or 1,024 different print formulas possible (more than a fourfold increase from three categories). Ask the students if this is a good reason to minimize the number of categories.

Behind The Scenes

Why are fingerprints taken?

Fingerprints form the basis for the most reliable system of identification in use today. Every person has a unique pattern of ridges on his fingertips. While hair color, appearance, weight, and height change over time, fingerprints stay virtually the same throughout a person's lifetime.

Sometimes fingerprints are left at the scene of a crime. Police compare these prints to the fingerprints of each suspect to see if they match. There are many other uses. For example, a child of unknown identity can be fingerprinted and those prints compared to the fingerprints of all missing children. High security workplaces, including some banks, military bases, and government buildings, have computers that check the fingerprints of employees at the entrance to the building.

Has fingerprinting always been used for identification?

Fingerprints have been recorded for thousands of years. The Babylonians recorded their fingerprints in soft clay as a safeguard against forgery. In ancient China and Japan, fingerprints were used as signatures. Stone carvings have been found in Canada that depict fingerprint patterns. These carvings are thought to pre-date the Europeans' arrival in North America. However, it's only been in the last century that an organized system of fingerprinting has been used in crime detection.

Fingerprints can be an important component in understanding genetics and multifactorial inheritance. A larger area of study, dermatoglyphics, which includes the study of dermal ridge patterns and flexion creases on the digits, palms, and soles, is useful in the clinical diagnosis of chromosome abnormalities.

The first widely used descriptive identification system was the Bertillon system of criminal identification. Used before the turn of the century, the Bertillon system relied on a series of descriptions and measurements of the body. Such facts as the size of the ear, the length and breadth of the skull, and the length of the little and middle fingers were recorded along with over 200 other precise measurements that characterized what were considered to be the unchanging features of a person's physical appearance. The Bertillon system was eventually abandoned in favor of the fingerprint classification system, developed in about 1880 by Francis Galton, a cousin of Charles Darwin.

What other systems of identification are used by criminalists?

Criminalists collect and compare hair samples, blood type, voice prints, handwriting, and other descriptive characteristics of human beings. While some of these forms of evidence are legally valid, none are as conclusive as the positive identification of fingerprints.

Is there something like a fingerprint system for animals?

While most animals don't have fingers, systems for identifying animals have been developed. For instance, owners of valuable horses have nose prints of their horses made so they can identify the horse in the event that it is stolen. Marine biologists identify whales by the pattern of barnacles found on their flukes, or tails.

Do the police use the arch-loop-whorl fingerprint classification system?

The standard three-category classification system used in this guide is a simplified version of the system used by professional criminalists. In addition to what is referred to as the plain arch, there is a tented arch. There is a left loop, a right loop, a double loop, and what's called a central pocket loop. There is a plain whorl, and then the composite category that we call "mixed," which criminalists sometimes refer to as an accidental whorl.

What other features are used to characterize fingerprints?

The police will often have only a single fingerprint from which to identify a person. Sometimes, that print won't even be complete. Criminalists must rely on a number of fingerprint features besides the fingerprint classification to characterize that print. Line features they typically look for include: a line with an abrupt ending; a y-shaped intersection of two lines; forked intersections of lines, scars, and wrinkles.

Who keeps track of fingerprints?

The Department of Justice began a fingerprint file in the early 1900 s. The Federal Bureau of Investigation subsequently began a fingerprint file in about 1930, which is now considered to be the largest collection of fingerprints in the world. Government employees, military personnel, and people in many other occupations are required to be fingerprinted. Many states require that all licensed drivers have a thumbprint on file. People are routinely fingerprinted when they are arrested. Many children are fingerprinted. Sometimes their parents keep their fingerprints. In other instances, their prints are put in a central file.

Fingerprint ridge details are also studied in the crime lab. There will always be slight differences in different fingerprint impressions of the same finger. However, if a sufficient number of matching ridge details appear in the same relative location in two different fingerprint impressions, it can be concluded that the prints are from the same source. In the United States, any combination of twelve such details is considered sufficient to associate a fingerprint impression with a particular finger. Magnification is often used to observe and compare ridge details carefully. The diagram shows the ten main ridge details, listed in their order of frequency, beginning with the most frequent, an "ending ridge."

1. ENDING RIDGE

2. FORK

3. SHORT RIDGE

4. DOT

5. BRIDGE

6. HOOK

7. EYE

8. DOUBLE FORK

9. DELTA

10. TRIPLE FORK

Recent innovations have allowed law enforcement agencies to use computers to search through fingerprint files. These computers can examine and compare as many fingerprints in an afternoon as a human criminalist could in a lifetime!

How do the police remove fingerprints from the scene of a crime?

Sometimes visible prints are left at the scene of a crime, allowing police to photograph the pattern that is left behind. More commonly, invisible or "latent" prints are left on objects.

Latent prints found on non-absorbent surfaces, such as wood or metal, can be dusted with colored powder. The powder sticks to the perspiration and skin oils that were left behind. The powdered pattern is lifted with transparent tape and then photographed.

A different treatment must be used to detect latent prints left on absorbent surfaces, like paper or cloth. Chemicals that react with substances in perspiration to form a colored image are applied to the absorbent surface. These chemically "developed" prints are then photographed. Alternatively, a laser can be used to cause perspiration to shine with a yellow color when photographed.

How are fingerprints formed?

Fingerprints are formed before birth. By the time a fetus is 11 weeks old, the first gentle ridges have formed on its fingers. One of the deepest layers of skin pushes upwards, making ripples in the layers of skin above it. By the time a baby is born, there are seven layers of skin. The fingerprint ridges ripple through the top five layers of skin.

One recommended adult reference book is Criminalistics: An Introduction to Forensic Science by Richard Saferstein (4th edition), Prentice Hall, 1990. There is also an accompanying lab manual.

Can a person change or remove her fingerprints?

Because fingerprints penetrate through five layers of skin, they are nearly impossible to obliterate, though notorious criminals have often tried, using metal files and acid treatments. Removing one's fingerprints requires surgically removing the fingertip and replacing it with skin grafted from another part of the body. Even after this complicated surgery is done, the ridges on the side of the finger can often still be seen.

What training does a person need to become a crime lab scientist?

To become a criminalist or forensic scientist, one usually needs a degree in criminalistics, chemistry, or a related field. Police officers sometimes receive special training to become fingerprint specialists.

Genetic "fingerprinting" has received a great deal of attention as laboratory techniques for analysis of DNA become more sophisticated, reliable, and widespread. The use of the term "fingerprinting" is of course not meant literally. Each of us, except for identical twins, carries a unique genetic pattern in our DNA. DNA "fingerprinting" has been accepted as evidence in some courtroom and legal situations, although not yet universally. Reliability and standardization of testing procedures remain issues, and there are concerns related to the possible greater commonalities of genetic characteristics in smaller ethnic and religious groups who have tended to intermarry. There is an excellent and detailed article on "Genetic Fingerprinting" by Pauline Lowrie and Susan Wells in New Scientist magazine, Number 52, November 16, 1991. The article explains what a DNA fingerprint is, and how it is recorded as patterns in a gel (somewhat similar to the chromatography techniques in the GEMS guide Crime Lab Chemistry). The article also explains the use of DNA fingerprinting in the identification of rapists, other legal and medical applications, and discusses reliability controversies. The article concludes, "Many more applications for DNA fingerprinting will no doubt be developed. Indeed, one day hospitals may take DNA fingerprints of all newborn babies and store the information on computer, turning each person's genetic material into the ultimate, lifelong identity card." There is also an article in the New Scientist of March 31, 1990 entitled "Is DNA Fingerprinting Ready for the Courts?" The GEMS guide Mystery Festival will include more background information on DNA fingerprinting, as one of the learning stations older students use to try to solve the "Felix mystery" involves DNA testing.

Summary Outlines

Session 1: Making Fingerprints

Getting Ready Before the Activity
1. Assemble the materials.
2. Duplicate the "Your Fingerprints" sheets.
3. Spend 5-10 minutes practicing the fingerprinting technique.

Introducing the Activity
1. Lead a short discussion about fingerprints.
2. Explain that the students will be criminalists.

Practicing Making Prints
1. Demonstrate the fingerprinting technique.
2. Let the students practice.

Making a Clean Set of Fingerprints
1. Explain the "Your Fingerprints" sheet.
2. Help the students make fingerprints.
3. Pass out magnifying lenses.
4. Collect the data sheets.

Session 2: Classifying Fingerprints

Getting Ready Before the Activity
1. Assemble the materials.
2. Duplicate the "10 Fingerprints" and the "Fingerprint Patterns" sheets.
3. Make an overhead transparency of the "Fingerprint Patterns" sheet.
4. Cut out sets of ten fingerprints and put them in envelopes.
5. Familiarize yourself with the fingerprint classification scheme.

Students Create Their Own Fingerprint Classifications

1. Review the last session.
2. Divide the class into teams of two.
3. Show the envelope of prints and ask the students to think of words to describe the patterns they see.
4. Distribute the envelopes containing sets of fingerprints and the magnifying lenses.
5. Record the responses on the chalkboard.
6. Ask the students to sort the prints according to patterns.
7. Summarize their classifications on the board.

Learning the Standard Fingerprint Classification System

1. Use the overhead to define the three basic patterns.
2. Answer questions about the standard classification system.

Applying the Standard Classification

1. Have the class use the standard classification to sort the ten fingerprints.
2. List the prints under the chalkboard headings, "arch," "loop," and "whorl."
3. Lead a short discussion to clarify the categories.

Finding Their Own Fingerprint Formulas

1. Hand back the "Your Fingerprints" data sheet from Session 1.
2. Have the students classify their own fingerprints.
3. Explain the fingerprint formula and have the students figure out theirs.
4. List a few students' fingerprint formulas.

Session 3: Solving the Crime

Getting Ready Before the Activity
Duplicate the "Suspects" and "Safe With Prints" sheets.

Who Robbed the Safe?
1. Tell the story.
2. Explain that they are to figure out the suspects' fingerprint formulas.
3. Reveal the fingerprint formula found on the safe.
4. Let the students speculate as to which suspect's fingerprints might be on the safe.
5. Distribute the "Safe With Prints" sheet.
6. Ask the students to decide whose prints they are.

Wrapping Up the Evidence
1. Let the students report whose fingerprints match those on the safe.
2. Encourage the students to imagine the many reasons that the safe might have these particular prints on it.
3. Ask what other techniques they could use to help solve the crime.

Literature Connections

Several of the books listed below explore how **footprints** can be used as clues to the identities of the animals who left them. The rest of the books are **mysteries**, some of which involve the technique of **fingerprinting**. In the GEMS literature handbook, *Once Upon A GEMS Guide: Connecting Young People's Literature to Great Explorations in Math and Science*, you might also find good literature connections listed under the GEMS guide *Crime Lab Chemistry*, as well as the science theme of "Diversity and Unity" and the math strands of "Logic" and "Pattern." The mysteries listed here, as most mysteries do, involve the discovery of **evidence** and its subsequent analysis to make **inferences**. The GEMS guides *Investigating Artifacts* (published in 1992) and *Mystery Festival* (scheduled to be available by late 1993) further explore evidence and inference.

Some teachers also use newspaper articles that describe a crime (usually unsolved), the evidence involved and some possible inferences. See "Assessment Suggestions" in this teacher's guide for an activity of this kind that can be used as an assessment of student learning for this and/or the *Crime Lab Chemistry* GEMS unit. There are also books listed below that contain **non-fiction accounts of mysteries or scientific discoveries**, in which detective-like behavior is exemplified. Such a mystery would be particularly apt if it involved fingerprinting or what is currently called **DNA fingerprinting**. Students could also be asked to write the story of a great scientific discovery in typical mystery style.

For more advanced students, there are many excellent mysteries written for the adult audience that include much discussion of evidence and inference, the process of elimination and other logical reasoning processes, and the importance of forensic science and scientists.

Cam Jensen and the Mystery of the Gold Coins
by David A. Adler; illustrated by Susanna Natti
Viking Press, New York. 1982
Dell Publishing, New York. 1984
Grades: 3–5

Cam Jensen uses her photographic memory to solve a theft of two gold coins. Cam and her friend Eric carry around their 5th grade science projects throughout the book and the final scenes take place at the school science fair. (Other titles in the series include *Cam Jensen and the Mystery at the Monkey House* and *Cam Jensen and the Mystery of the Dinosaur Bones* in which she notices that three bones are missing from a museum's mounted dinosaur.)

Chip Rogers: Computer Whiz
by Seymour Simon; illustrated by Steve Miller
William Morrow, New York. 1984
Out of print
Grades: 4–8

Two youngsters, a boy and a girl, solve a gem theft from a science museum by using a computer to classify clues. A computer is also used to weigh variables in choosing a basketball team. Although some details about programming the computer may be a little dated, this is still a good book revolving directly around sorting out evidence, deciding whether or not a crime has been committed, solving it, and demonstrating the role computers can play in human endeavors. By the author of the Einstein Anderson series.

From the Mixed-Up Files of Mrs. Basil E. Frankweiler
written and illustrated by E.L. Konigsburg
Atheneum, New York. 1967
Dell Publishing, New York. 1977
Grades: 5–8

> Twelve-year-old Claudia and her younger brother run away from home to live in the Metropolitan Museum of Art and stumble upon a mystery involving a statue attributed to Michelangelo. This book is a classic, and has been recommended to GEMS by many teachers. Because the detecting techniques used include fingerprinting and chromatography it is a particularly apt connection to *Crime Lab Chemistry* and *Fingerprinting*.

The Great Adventures of Sherlock Holmes
by Arthur Conan Doyle
Viking Penguin, New York. 1990
Grades: 6–Adult

> These classic short stories are masterly examples of deduction. Many of the puzzling cases are solved by Holmes in his chemistry lab as he analyzes fingerprints, inks, tobaccos, mud, etc. to solve the crime and catch the criminal. These stories are available from many different publishers and in many editions.

Let's Go Dinosaur Tracking
by Miriam Schlein; illustrated by Kate Duke
HarperCollins, New York. 1991
Grades: 2–5

> The many different types of tracks dinosaurs left behind and what these giant steps reveal is explored. Was the creature running … chasing a lizard … browsing on its hind legs for leaves … traveling in pairs or in a pack … walking underwater? At the end of the book, you can measure your stride and compare the difference when walking slowly, walking fast, and running. The process involved in attempting to draw conclusions about an animal's behavior or movement patterns from its tracks is similar to the way inferences are drawn from evidence in the GEMS mystery-solving activities. You could discuss with your students how they would weigh the evidence and consider the suspects if, for example, muddy shoeprints of a suspect had also been found at the scene of the crime.

The Mystery of the Stranger in the Barn
by True Kelley
Dodd, Mead, & Co., New York. 1986
Grades: K–4

> A discarded hat and disappearing objects seem to prove that a mysterious stranger is hiding out in the barn, but no one ever sees anyone. A good opportunity to contrast evidence and inference.

The One Hundredth Thing About Caroline
by Lois Lowry
Houghton Mifflin, Boston. 1983
Dell Publishing, New York. 1991
Grades: 5–9

> Fast-moving and often humorous book about 11-year-old Caroline, an aspiring
> paleontologist, and her friend Stacy's attempts to conduct investigations.
> Caroline becomes convinced that a neighbor has ominous plans to "eliminate"
> the children and Stacy speculates about the private life of a famous neighbor.
> Due to hasty misinterpretations of real evidence, both prove to be wildly wrong
> in their inferences. Gathering evidence, weighing it, and deciding what makes
> sense are good accompanying themes. A somewhat inaccurate portrayal of
> "color blindness" is a minor flaw.

Susannah and the Blue House Mystery
by Patricia Elmore
E.P. Dutton, New York. 1980
Scholastic, New York. 1990
Grades: 5–7

> Susannah (an amateur herpetologist) and Lucy have formed a detective agency.
> They check into the death of a kindly old antique dealer who lived in the
> mysterious "Blue House." They attempt to piece together clues in hopes of
> finding the treasure they think he has left to one of them. The detectives evaluate
> evidence, work together to solve problems, and prevent a camouflaged theft
> from taking place.

Susannah and the Poison Green Halloween
by Patricia Elmore
E.P. Dutton, New York. 1982
Scholastic., New York. 1990
Grades: 5–7

> Susannah and her friends try to figure out who put the poison in their Halloween
> candy when they trick-or-treated at the Eucalyptus Arms apartments. Tricky
> clues, changing main suspects, and some medical chemistry make this an
> excellent choice, with lots of inference and mystery.

Who Really Killed Cock Robin?
by Jean Craighead George
HarperCollins, New York. 1991
Grades: 3–7

> A compelling ecological mystery examines the importance of keeping nature in
> balance, and provides an inspiring account of a young environmental hero who
> becomes a scientific detective.

Whose Footprints?
by Masayuki Yabuuchi
Philomel Books, New York. 1983
Grades: K–4

> A good guessing game for younger students that depicts the footprints of a duck,
> cat, bear, horse, hippopotamus, and goat.

Assessment Suggestions

5th Grade GEMS Crime Lab Science Assessment

Comparing Fingerprints

Purpose: The student demonstrates mastery of the graphite-tape fingerprinting technique, and comfort in using rich attribute vocabulary to describe her own thumbprint and another print. She demonstrates her ability to compare two prints and describe their differences and their similarities. The task provides an opportunity to use the classifications of arch, loop, whorl in context.

When: The task could be administered after completion of the GEMS "Crime Lab Science" guides (*Fingerprinting* and *Crime Lab Chemistry*). Or, it could be administered after just the GEMS *Fingerprinting* activities.

The Task: The teacher provides each group of students with a roll of the same kind of transparent tape used in the Fingerprinting unit, scratch paper, magnifying lenses, and a # 2 pencil for each student. Students complete the student sheet on "Comparing Fingerprints." (Note: The sheet should be duplicated at high enough quality so the lines of the fingerprint are clearly discernible. Do not mimeograph.) The task involves students in using the tape and graphite method to take their own thumbprint, and in using attribute vocabulary to describe their own thumbprint and another one on the page, then describe how the two are different and similar. The teacher provides students with oral or written feedback on their answers.

Evaluation: The teacher scores student responses based on: the degree to which students are able to make a clear thumbprint; the richness of the attribute vocabulary used by the student; the kind and number of similarities and differences listed; and the degree of ability to make correct references to the formal classifications of arch, loop, and whorl.

Please see page 46 for a summary of selected student learning outcomes, with built-in and additional assessment suggestions, for this GEMS *Fingerprinting* guide. To learn more about the assessment of inquiry-based science and mathematics, we recommend the GEMS assessment handbook, entitled *Insights and Outcomes: Assessments for Great Explorations in Math and Science.* The handbook includes selected student outcomes for all GEMS teacher's guides. It features case studies with actual student work to highlight different assessment strategies and evaluation techniques. A real-life introduction tells the story of one year in the life of two teachers who are grappling with issues of assessment. The GEMS assessment handbook is available from GEMS. See the inside back cover of this guide for a listing of all guides and handbooks, along with our address and phone number.

Name _____   Date _____

Comparing Fingerprints

Use tape and a pencil to make a print of your thumb. (Your
choice of left or right.) Put the print in the empty box below:

In the space below, use words to describe the
patterns and lines you see in this print.
List as many descriptions as you can!

_____

_____

_____

_____

_____

_____

In the space below, use words to describe the
patterns and lines you see in this print.
List as many descriptions as you can!

_____

_____

_____

_____

_____

_____

Tell how these two fingerprints are different:

_____

_____

_____

_____

Tell how these two fingerprints are alike:

_____

_____

_____

_____

5th Grade GEMS Crime Lab Science Assessment

Newspaper Article Critique and Review

Purpose: The student demonstrates that she can identify fact and inference in a newspaper article and is able to rewrite the article to reduce the number of erroneous inferences.

When: The task should be administered after completion of the GEMS "Crime Lab Science" guides (*Fingerprinting* and *Crime Lab Chemistry*).

The Task: The teacher reads a scenario out loud, about a possible arson incident. With a written version of the scenario, the students are asked to identify the unfair inferences made in a newspaper article about the situation and then to rewrite the article to better reflect the facts and avoid unfair inferences. The teacher provides the students with oral or written feedback on their responses.

Evaluation & Documentation: The teacher scores the students' responses based on whether or not and how fully the student demonstrates competence in identifying unfair or incorrect inferences, and whether or not and to what extent the rewrite: is based on evidence/fact; includes more details about the situation; and (if the rewrite includes an inference) whether or not and how the inference is qualified.

Crime Lab Chemistry is an excellent curricular "accomplice" to *Fingerprinting*.

Name _____   Date _____

Newspaper Article: Evidence or Inference?

Imagine that you are a news reporter:

You are assigned to write an article about a grass fire burning in a nearby town. You go to the burning field where fire fighters are trying to put out the fire. There are huge flames, but the fire chief tells you that the fire seems to be under control. This is lucky, because the field is next to an oil refinery. By asking more questions, you learn that there is some evidence that the fire was started on purpose.

You go to the police department's crime lab, and there you talk to the criminalist who is working on this case. You learn that a note was found nailed to a telephone pole next to the field. The note said, "The price of gas is too high. I'll make this company pay!!" Through chromatography tests, it was found that the note was written with a black NIKKO pen—a common brand of pen.

You go to the police station and there you find out that the police are questioning three suspects: a high school student who works at a local gas station owned by the company whose field was set on fire, a man who used to work for the oil company but lost his job, and the Mayor herself! All three of these people were seen near the field in the hour before the fire began. The Mayor had a black NIKKO brand pen with her when she was questioned; the other two didn't have black pens in their pockets. No arrests have been made in the case.

You come back to your office and you find that another reporter has already written an article about the fire. Your boss asks you to read it over and underline all the places where an unfair inference was made. Do that here:

Mayor Is Arrested for Arson!

A fire is burning out of control in a grassy field. Fire fighters are

worried that a neighboring oil refinery may burn down. The

Mayor was seen nailing something to a telephone pole near the

grassy field. A note found on the telephone pole was written with

the Mayor's pen. According to the police, there are two other

suspects, but they probably didn't light the fire.

Seeing that the other reporter made unfair inferences, your boss asks you to rewrite the article so it is more true. Rewrite the article changing any words or phrases that are not based on fact or evidence.

Assessment Suggestions

Selected Student Outcomes

1. Students develop rich attribute vocabulary to describe fingerprint patterns.

2. Students articulate similarities and differences between fingerprints.

3. Students use the standard arch-loop-whorl system to classify fingerprints.

4. Students improve their ability to distinguish evidence from inference.

Built-In Assessment Activity

Solving the Crime: In Session 3, Solving the Crime, students use the standard arch-loop-whorl fingerprint classification system to solve a mystery and make inferences. During the session, the teacher can observe how students apply the standard classification system for each suspect. The evidence that students use to support their inference is also observable. (Outcomes 3, 4)

Additional Assessment Ideas

Newspaper Article: Evidence or Inference? Students are asked to rewrite an article about a grass fire to correct the unfair inferences that are made. See pages 44 and 45 of this guide for a description of the assessment task and a sample article. You may want to adapt the article to include more fingerprinting information. (Outcome 4)

News Reporters: In the Going Further activity for Session 3, students are invited to write newspaper articles about the crime, draw pictures, and create stories about the suspects. Teachers can ask half of the students to write their stories based on evidence, where any inference made is qualified. The other half of the class can be asked to write their stories for a tabloid newspaper, where evidence is secondary and wild inferences are welcome. Selected articles can then be read aloud, and the class can determine whether the article is based mostly on evidence or mostly on unfair inference. Individual papers and class discussion provide the "evidence" on which the teacher can assess students' ability to distinguish factual evidence from unfair inference. (Outcome 4)

Fingerprint Comparison: Have students use the tape and graphite method to make their own thumbprint and use attribute vocabulary to describe it. They then compare their thumbprint to another print on the page and describe how the two are similar and different. This task provides the teacher with the opportunity to observe: students' mastery of the graphite-tape technique, ability to use rich attribute vocabulary, ability to compare two prints, and whether students are able to use the classifications of arch, loop, and whorl in context. Please see pages 42 and 43 for more detail. (Outcomes 1, 2, 3)

Guess Whose Thumb! The teacher secretly makes a copy of a student's thumb (from the data sheet in Session 1) and invites the class to ask "yes" or "no" questions to see if the thumbprint is theirs. This activity gives the teacher an opportunity to hear how students articulate descriptive vocabulary, describe similarities and differences, and to find out whether students use arch-loop-whorl vocabulary to help communicate during the task. (Outcomes 1, 2, 3)

My Thumb: Before and after the unit, students make a print of their own thumbs and write about the patterns they see. The teacher can observe how the students' descriptions change and what vocabulary they use to describe their thumbs. (Outcomes 1, 3)

Your Fingerprints

Name _____

Use this sheet with your right hand (palm down) or
your left hand (palm up).

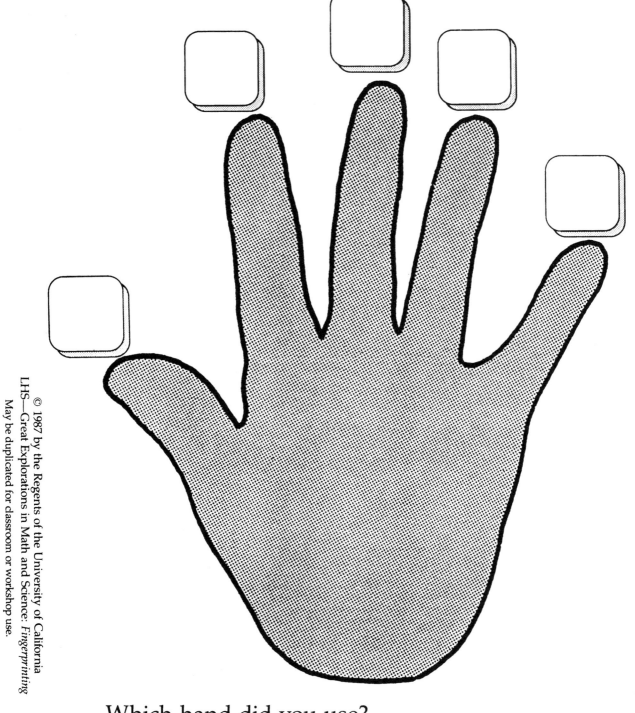

Which hand did you use? _____

What is your fingerprint formula? _____

10 Fingerprints

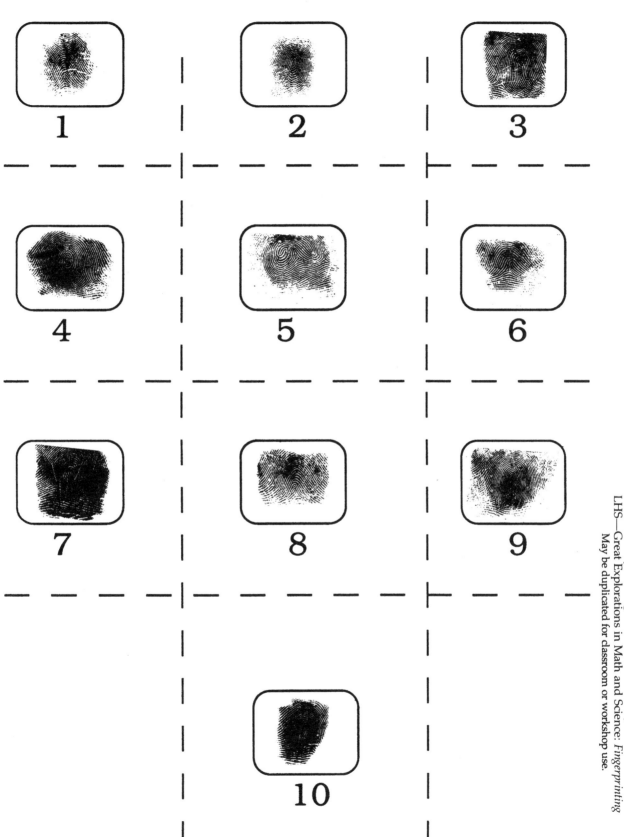

Suspects

An Example →

Arch	Loop	Whorl

	Thumb	Forefinger	Middle finger	Ring finger	Little finger
President			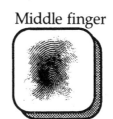		
Secretary					
Vice-President					
Accountant					
Janitor					

Suspects

Name _____

An Example ➜

Arch   Loop   Whorl

Thumb   Forefinger   Middle finger   Ring finger   Little finger

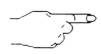 # Fingerprint Patterns

Every person in the world has a unique set of fingerprints, unlike those of any other person who ever lived.

Even though everyone's fingerprints are unique, there are basic patterns that are always found. These patterns help criminalists classify fingerprints.

The three basic patterns are:

Whorl patterns have lots of circles that **do not leave** either side of the print.

Arch patterns have lines that start on one side of the print, rise toward the center, and leave on the **other** side of the print.

Loop patterns have lines that start on one side of the print, rise toward the center, turn back and leave on the **same** side from which they started.

Whorl

Arch

Loop

Safe with prints

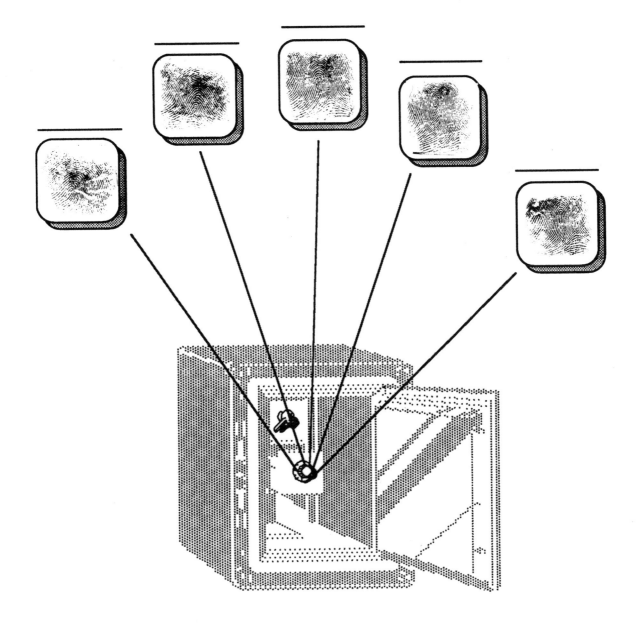